MW01132751

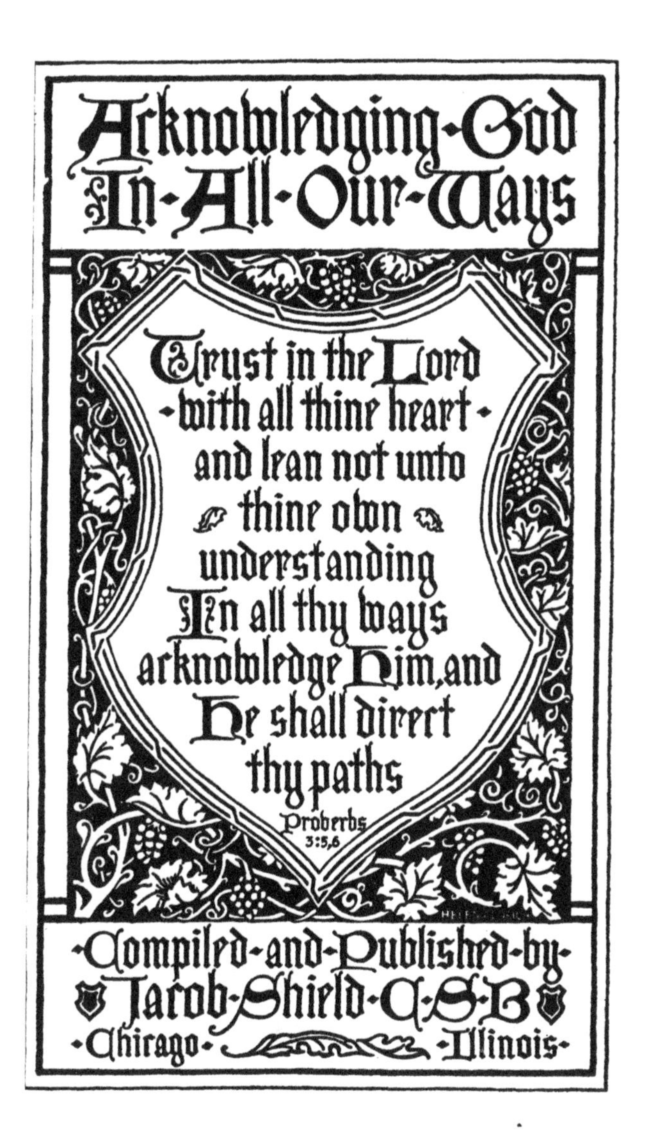
Acknowledging·God
In·All·Our·Ways
Trust in the Lord
·with all thine heart·
and lean not unto
thine own
understanding
In all thy ways
acknowledge Him, and
He shall direct
thy paths
Proverbs
3:5,6
·Compiled·and·Published·by·
Jacob·Shield·C·S·B
·Chicago· ·Illinois·

# FOREWORD

A NUMBER of years ago the writer began an analytical study of the Bible. In the first days of such study it seemed to him that one would need to have a life-long religious training in order to spiritualize thought, and as many of his years had been spent in acquiring material business and knowledge and seeking human pleasure, he felt a great sense of regret and discouragement because there appeared to be no probability of his ever attaining a spiritual consciousness.

One evening, while lamenting on what seemed a lost opportunity, he opened the Bible and began to read. His attention was attracted to the third chapter of Proverbs and in particular to verses five and six: "Trust in the Lord with all thine heart; and lean not unto thine own understanding. In all thy ways acknowledge Him, and He shall direct thy paths." An extraordinary fascination held him to these verses and he meditated upon and analyzed them for a long time in an effort to learn the reason for his unusual interest. It then occurred to him that they might be the key to the solution of his redemption from material thinking and its consequent difficulties, and he concluded to follow the instruction in those two verses—to acknowledge God in all his ways and not to trust in his own false understanding. As a result he persisted in declaring God the only Intelligence and Power that enabled him to think, to talk, to walk, to act, and in fact to do anything, however small or great. In every detail he accepted the conclusion that God was directing him in all his ways.

After having continued in this way of thinking for a brief period, he realized that his whole state of being was undergoing a marked change—thought was turning to spiritual things and the material was becoming secondary. He had a strong desire to eliminate all sinful thoughts from consciousness; he felt inclined toward loving, forgiving, kind, compassionate, and charitable thinking, and he wanted to be scrupulously honest in all his dealings. The result was that his health and appearance rapidly improved; fear diminished, and a feeling of strength and dominion came to him. His whole perspective of life changed and a longing to heal the sick, to comfort the sorrowing, and to help those in adversity, took possession of him. Soon these spiritual faculties asserted themselves and healings took place in a pronounced degree.

From that time to the present he has encouraged others to use these two verses in Proverbs and the purpose of this booklet is to amplify this interpretation so that the reader may get the broadest possible view of the extent to which these divine precepts may be employed in every-day experience.

The book has no other object and should not be considered in any other light.

The Bible quotations following the statements at the top of the pages are but a few of those which have been especially helpful in substantiating the divine authority and maintaining and proving the practicability of acknowledging God in all ways.

It is the fond hope of the author that all who will use these verses in the way here described, may have the same blessed experience that he has had, and to this result this booklet is lovingly dedicated.

JACOB SHIELD

# GOD IS MY ALL-IN-ALL

## ALL MATERIALITY AND MORTALITY ARE ILLUSIVE

In making such positive and negative statements as the above, it is not intended to convey the idea that material things, including sin, sickness and death, do not seem real—quite the contrary. They seem to be dense convictions. The contention between the positives (the real) and negatives (the unreal) is based on the truth of the divine Mind in contradistinction to the falsity of the human or mortal mind.

The human consciousness has been trained to think adversely regarding God, man, and the universe, due to idolatry, sorcery, astrology, witchcraft, superstition, false theology, material medical practice, etc. It will require time and great effort to eradicate the false impressions left by these ancient and modern delusions. The overcoming of them is well on the way and the realization of God's omnipotence, omniscience and omnipresence will eventually eliminate all else and the victory over sin, sickness and death will be won.

A study of the textbook of Christian Science, "Science and Health with Key to the Scriptures," by Mary Baker Eddy, will greatly aid the reader in comprehending the difference between the divine and human qualities of thought and will help him prove by demonstration the verity of the statements in this booklet.

That credit may be given where credit is due, it is only right to add that the desire to study the Scriptures and to comprehend their spiritual significance came to the author through Christian Science. Many years of active and continuous experience in and observation of this Science have convinced him beyond any possible doubt that it is the universal divine panacea and the restoration of all fundamental law, science and religion, which was introduced in the Old Testament, fulfilled and demonstrated in the New Testament, and lastly discovered, clarified and made available to all humanity by Mrs. Eddy in Christian Science.

# GOD IS MY LIFE

## THERE IS NO DEATH

**Bible:**

AND I give unto them eternal life; and they shall never perish, neither shall any *man* pluck them out of my hand. (John 10:28)

FOR as the Father hath life in himself; so hath he given to the Son to have life in himself; (John 5:26)

* * * he giveth to all life, and breath, and all things; (Acts 17:25)

AND this is the record, that God hath given to us eternal life, and this life is in his Son. (I John 5:11)

# GOD IS MY TRUTH

## THERE IS NO ERROR

**Bible:**

FOR the word of the Lord *is* right; and all his works *are done* in truth. (Ps. 33:4)

* * * his truth *shall be thy* shield and buckler. (Ps. 91:4)

* * * the truth of the Lord *endureth* for ever. * * * (Ps. 117:2)

THY word *is* true *from* the beginning: and every one of thy righteous judgments *endureth* for ever. (Ps. 119:160)

* * * *thy* counsels * * * *are* faithfulness *and* truth. (Isa. 25:1)

* * * I *am* the Lord — * * * That frustrateth the tokens of the liars, * * * (Isa. 44:24,25)

# GOD IS MY LOVE

## THERE IS NO MORTAL LOVE

**Bible:**

AS the Father hath loved me, so have I loved you: * * * (John 15:9)

* * * love is of God; * * * (I John 4:7)

* * * the God of love and peace shall be with you. (II Cor. 13:11)

* * * Thou shalt love the Lord thy God with all thy heart, and with all thy soul, and with all thy strength, and with all thy mind; * * * (Luke 10:27)

* * * he that loveth me shall be loved of my Father, and I will love him, and will manifest myself to him. (John 14:21)

* * * I have loved thee with an everlasting love: * * * (Jer. 31:3)

# GOD IS MY SPIRIT

## THERE IS NO EVIL SPIRIT

**Bible:**

* * * thou *art* my God: thy spirit *is* good; * * * (Ps. 143:10)

* * * behold, I will pour out my spirit unto you, * * * (Prov. 1:23)

AND the spirit of the Lord shall rest upon him, the spirit of wisdom and understanding, the spirit of counsel and might, the spirit of knowledge and of the fear of the Lord; (Isa. 11:2)

* * * I have put my spirit upon him: * * *(Isa. 42:1)

* * * My spirit that *is* upon thee, and my words which I have put in thy mouth, shall not depart out of thy mouth, * * * (Isa. 59:21)

# GOD IS MY MIND

## THERE IS NO MORTAL MIND

**Bible:**

* * * we have the mind of Christ. (I Cor. 2:16)

BUT without thy mind would I do nothing; * * * (Ph'm 1:14)

* * * I will put my laws into their mind, * * * (Heb. 8:10)

* * * put off concerning the former conversation the old man, which is corrupt according to the deceitful lusts;—And be renewed in the spirit of your mind;—* * * put on the new man, which after God is created in righteousness and true holiness. (Eph. 4:22,23,24)

# GOD IS MY SOUL

## THERE IS NO MATERIAL SENSE

**Bible:**

* * * my soul shall live because of thee. (Gen. 12:13)

* * * my soul shall be joyful in the Lord: it shall rejoice in his salvation. (Ps. 35:9)

TAKE my yoke upon you, and learn of me; for I am meek and lowly in heart: and ye shall find rest unto your souls. (Matt. 11:29)

HE maketh me to lie down in green pastures: he leadeth me beside the still waters.—He restoreth my soul: * * * (Ps. 23:2,3)

AS the hart panteth after the water brooks, so panteth my soul after thee, O God.—My soul thirsteth for God, for the living God: * * * (Ps. 42:1,2)

# GOD IS MY PRINCIPLE

## THERE IS NO DISORDER

**Bible:**

OF old hast thou laid the foundation of the earth: and the heavens *are* the work of thy hands. (Ps. 102:25)

AS the whirlwind passeth, so *is* the wicked no *more*: but the righteous *is* an everlasting foundation. (Prov. 10:25)

MINE hand also hath laid the foundation of the earth, and my right hand hath spanned the heavens: *when* I call unto them, they stand up together. (Isa. 48:13)

* * * the foundation of God standeth sure, * * * (II Tim. 2:19)

# GOD IS MY FATHER-MOTHER

## THERE IS NO HUMAN PARENTAGE

**Bible:**

**AND he answered them, saying, Who is my mother, or my brethren?—And he looked round about on them which sat about him, and said, Behold my mother and my brethren!—For whosoever shall do the will of God, the same is my brother, and my sister, and mother. (Mark 3:33,34,35)**

**HE shall cry unto me, Thou *art* my father, my God, and the rock of my salvation. (Ps. 89:26)**

*** * * call no *man* your father upon the earth: for one is your Father, which is in heaven. (Matt. 23:9)**

**SAY unto wisdom, Thou *art* my sister; and call understanding *thy* kinswoman: (Prov. 7:4)**

# GOD IS MY LIGHT

## THERE IS NO DARKNESS

**Bible:**

* * * the Lord shall be unto thee an everlasting light, * * * (Isa. 60:19)

* * * God is light, and in him is no darkness at all. (I John 1:5)

THEN spake Jesus again unto them, saying, I am the light of the world: he that followeth me shall not walk in darkness, but shall have the light of life. (John 8:12)

* * * the darkness is past, and the true light now shineth. (I John 2:8)

FOR with thee *is* the fountain of life: in thy light shall we see light. (Ps. 36:9)

THE Lord *is* my light and my salvation; * * * (Ps. 27:1)

# GOD IS MY WISDOM

## THERE IS NO IGNORANCE

**Bible:**

FOR the Lord giveth wisdom: out of his mouth *cometh* knowledge and understanding. (Prov. 2:6)

FOR I will give you a mouth and wisdom, which all your adversaries shall not be able to gainsay nor resist. (Luke 21:15)

THERE *is* no wisdom nor understanding nor counsel against the Lord. (Prov. 21:30)

IN whom are hid all the treasures of wisdom and knowledge. (Col. 2:3)

FOR the wisdom of this world is foolishness with God. * * * (I Cor. 3:19)

# GOD IS MY LAW

## THERE IS NO MORTAL MIND LAW

**Bible:**

* * * I will put my law in their inward parts, and write it in their hearts; * * * (Jer. 31:33)

FOR the Lord *is* our judge, the Lord *is* our lawgiver, the Lord *is* our king; he will save us. (Isa. 33:22)

FOR the law of the Spirit of life in Christ Jesus hath made me free from the law of sin and death. (Rom. 8:2)

* * * a law shall proceed from me, and I will make my judgment to rest for a light of the people. (Isa. 51:4)

FOR we know that the law is spiritual: * * * (Rom. 7:14)

* * * it is easier for heaven and earth to pass, than one tittle of the law to fail. (Luke 16:17)

# GOD IS MY PROVIDER

## THERE IS NO LIMITATION

**Bible:**

* * * Son, thou art ever with me, and all that I have is thine. (Luke 15:31)

BUT my God shall supply all your need according to his riches in glory by Christ Jesus. (Phil. 4:19)

BEHOLD the fowls of the air: for they sow not, neither do they reap, nor gather into barns; yet your heavenly Father feedeth them. Are ye not much better than they? (Matt. 6:26)

ASK, and it shall be given you; seek, and ye shall find; knock, and it shall be opened unto you:—Or what man is there of you, whom if his son ask bread, will he give him a stone?—Or if he ask a fish, will he give him a serpent?—If ye then, being evil, know how to give good gifts unto your children, how much more shall your Father which is in heaven give good things to them that ask him? (Matt. 7:7,9,10,11)

# GOD IS MY COURAGE

## THERE IS NO DISCOURAGEMENT

**Bible:**

WAIT on the Lord: be of good courage, and he shall strengthen thine heart: wait, I say, on the Lord. (Ps. 27:14)

* * * in the hearts of all that are wise hearted I have put wisdom, that they may make all that I have commanded thee; (Ex. 31:6)

BEHOLD, the Lord thy God hath set the land before thee: go up *and* possess *it*, as the Lord God of thy fathers hath said unto thee; fear not, neither be discouraged. (Deut. 1:21)

THOU shalt not be affrighted at them: for the Lord thy God *is* among you, * * * (Deut. 7:21)

IN whom we have boldness and access with confidence by the faith of him. (Eph. 3:12)

# GOD IS MY JOY

## THERE IS NO SORROW

**Bible:**

* * * your heart shall rejoice, and your joy no man taketh from you. (John 16:22)

* * * thou shalt make me full of joy with thy countenance. (Acts 2:28)

* * * for *this* day *is* holy unto our Lord: neither be ye sorry; for the joy of the Lord is your strength. (Neh. 8:10)

* * * in thy presence *is* fulness of joy; at thy right hand *there are* pleasures for evermore. (Ps. 16:11)

* * * weeping may endure for a night, but joy *cometh* in the morning. (Ps. 30:5)

THE Lord hath done great things for us; *whereof* we are glad.—They that sow in tears shall reap in joy. (Ps. 126:3,5)

## GOD IS MY FRIEND

### THERE IS NO ENEMY

**Bible:**

AND the Lord spake unto Moses face to face, as a man speaketh unto his friend. * * * (Ex. 33:11)

A FRIEND loveth at all times, * * * (Prov. 17:17)

A MAN *that hath* friends must shew himself friendly: and there is a friend *that* sticketh closer than a brother. (Prov. 18:24)

HIS mouth *is* most sweet: yea, he *is* altogether lovely. This *is* my beloved, and this *is* my friend, O daughters of Jerusalem. (Song of Solomon 5:16)

BUT thou, Israel, *art* my servant, Jacob whom I have chosen, the seed of Abraham my friend. (Isa. 41:8)

## GOD IS MY COMPANION

### THERE IS NO LONELINESS

**Bible:**

I *AM* a companion of all *them* that fear thee, and of them that keep thy precepts. (Ps. 119:63)

WE took sweet counsel together, *and* walked unto the house of God in company. (Ps. 55:14)

GOD *is* faithful, by whom ye were called unto the fellowship of his Son Jesus Christ our Lord. (I Cor. 1:9)

BE ye not unequally yoked together with unbelievers: for what fellowship hath righteousness with unrighteousness? and what communion hath light with darkness? (II Cor. 6:14)

# GOD IS MY HUSBAND-WIFE

## THERE IS NO SINGLENESS

**Bible:**

FOR thy Maker *is* thine husband; the Lord of hosts *is* his name; * * * (Isa. 54:5)

* * * for I have espoused you to one husband, * * * (II Cor. 11:2)

AND I will betroth thee unto me for ever; * * * (Hos. 2:19)

NEVERTHELESS neither is the man without the woman, neither the woman without the man, in the Lord.—For as the woman *is* of the man, even so *is* the man also by the woman; but all things of God. (I Cor. 11:11,12)

# GOD IS MY HAPPINESS

## THERE IS NO DEPRESSION NOR DESPONDENCY

**Bible:**

BLESSED *is* every one that feareth the Lord; that walketh in his ways.—For thou shalt eat the labour of thine hands: happy *shalt* thou *be,* and *it shall be* well with thee. (Ps. 128:1,2)

HAST thou faith? have *it* to thyself before God. Happy *is* he that condemneth not himself in that thing which he alloweth. (Rom. 14:22)

BEHOLD, we count them happy which endure. Ye have heard of the patience of Job, and have seen the end of the Lord; that the Lord is very pitiful, and of tender mercy. (James 5:11)

HAPPY *is he* that *hath* the God of Jacob for his help, whose hope *is* in the Lord his God: (Ps. 146:5)

# GOD IS MY SATISFACTION

## THERE IS NO DISSATISFACTION

**Bible:**

AS for me, I will behold thy face in righteousness: I shall be satisfied, when I awake, with thy likeness. (Ps. 17:15)

MY soul shall be satisfied as *with* marrow and fatness; and my mouth shall praise *thee* with joyful lips: (Ps. 63:5)

THOU openest thine hand, and satisfiest the desire of every living thing. (Ps. 145:16)

FOR he satisfieth the longing soul, and filleth the hungry soul with goodness. (Ps. 107:9)

# GOD IS MY BLESSING

## THERE IS NO CURSE

**Bible:**

* * * the Lord thy God turned the curse into a blessing unto thee, because the Lord thy God loved thee. (Deut. 23:5)

THE blessing of the Lord, it maketh rich, and he addeth no sorrow with it. (Prov. 10:22)

A FAITHFUL man shall abound with blessings: * * * (Prov. 28:20)

FOR the Lord thy God blesseth thee, as he promised thee: * * * (Deut. 15:6)

THE Lord bless thee, and keep thee:—The Lord make his face shine upon thee, and be gracious unto thee:—The Lord lift up his countenance upon thee, and give thee peace. (Num. 6:24,25,26)

# GOD IS MY HOLINESS

## THERE IS NO UNGODLINESS

**Bible:**

WHO *is* like unto thee, O Lord, * * * who *is* like thee, glorious in holiness, fearful *in* praises, doing wonders? (Ex. 15:11)

GIVE unto the Lord the glory due unto his name; worship the Lord in the beauty of holiness. (Ps. 29:2)

O WORSHIP the Lord in the beauty of holiness: fear before him, all the earth. (Ps. 96:9)

SING unto the Lord, O ye saints of his, and give thanks at the remembrance of his holiness. (Ps. 30:4)

HAVING therefore these promises, dearly beloved, let us cleanse ourselves from all filthiness of the flesh and spirit, perfecting holiness in the fear of God. (II Cor. 7:1)

# GOD IS MY LOCOMOTION

## THERE IS NO ATAXIA

**Bible:**

* * * The Lord, before whom I walk, will send his angel with thee, and prosper thy way; * * * (Gen. 24:40)

I WILL walk before the Lord in the land of the living. (Ps. 116:9)

HE that walketh uprightly walketh surely: * * * (Prov. 10:9)

O HOUSE of Jacob, come ye, and let us walk in the light of the Lord. (Isa. 2:5)

THERE *is* therefore now no condemnation to them which are in Christ Jesus, who walk not after the flesh, but after the Spirit. (Rom. 8:1)

## GOD IS MY SUPPLY

### THERE IS NO WANT

**Bible:**

FOR I know that this shall turn to my salvation through your prayer, and the supply of the Spirit of Jesus Christ, (Phil. 1:19)

THEY shall be abundantly satisfied with the fatness of thy house; and thou shalt make them drink of the river of thy pleasures. (Ps. 36:8)

BUT seek ye first the kingdom of God, and his righteousness; and all these things shall be added unto you. (Matt. 6:33)

I WILL abundantly bless her provision: I will satisfy her poor with bread. (Ps. 132:15)

# GOD IS MY PROSPERITY

## THERE IS NO ADVERSITY

**Bible:**

AND in my prosperity I said, I shall never be moved.—Lord, by thy favour thou hast made my mountain to stand strong: * * * (Ps. 30:6,7)

DEPART from evil, and do good; and dwell for evermore.—For the Lord loveth judgment, and forsaketh not his saints; they are preserved for ever: but the seed of the wicked shall be cut off. (Ps. 37:27,28)

AND thus shall ye say to him that liveth *in prosperity,* Peace *be* both to thee, and peace *be* to thine house, and peace *be* unto all that thou hast. (I Sam. 25:6)

FOR the Lord God *is* a sun and shield: the Lord will give grace and glory: no good *thing* will he withhold from them that walk uprightly. (Ps. 84:11)

## GOD IS MY HELP

### THERE IS NO HELPLESSNESS

**Bible:**

OUR soul waiteth for the Lord: he *is* our help and our shield. (Ps. 33:20)

WHY art thou cast down, O my soul? and *why* art thou disquieted in me? hope thou in God: for I shall yet praise him *for* the help of his countenance. (Ps. 42:5)

GOD *is* our refuge and strength, a very present help in trouble. (Ps. 46:1)

I WILL lift up mine eyes unto the hills, from whence cometh my help.—My help *cometh* from the Lord, which made heaven and earth.—The sun shall not smite thee by day, nor the moon by night. (Ps. 121:1, 2,6)

# GOD IS MY JUDGE

## THERE IS NO INJUSTICE NOR PREJUDICE

**Bible:**

AND the heavens shall declare his righteousness: for God *is* judge himself. (Ps. 50:6)

* * * it is he which was ordained of God *to be* the Judge of quick and dead. (Acts 10:42)

HENCEFORTH there is laid up for me a crown of righteousness, which the Lord, the righteous judge, shall give me at that day: and not to me only, but unto all them also that love his appearing. (II Tim. 4:8)

FOR the time *is come* that judgment must begin at the house of God: and if *it* first *begin* at us, what shall the end *be* of them that obey not the gospel of God? (I Peter 4:17)

# GOD IS MY PROTECTOR

## THERE IS NO INSECURITY

**Bible:**

ABIDE thou with me, * * * with me thou *shalt be* in safeguard. (I Sam. 22:23)

AND thou shalt be secure, because there is hope; yea, thou shalt dig *about thee, and* thou shalt take thy rest in safety. (Job 11:18)

MY defence *is* of God, which saveth the upright in heart. (Ps. 7:10)

THE Lord *is* nigh unto them that are of a broken heart; and saveth such as be of a contrite spirit. (Ps. 34:18)

SAY to them *that are* of a fearful heart, Be strong, fear not: behold, your God will come * * * and save you. (Isa. 35:4)

# GOD IS MY COMFORTER

## THERE IS NO GRIEF

**Bible:**

YEA, though I walk through the valley of the shadow of death, I will fear no evil: for thou *art* with me; thy rod and thy staff they comfort me. (Ps. 23:4)

THOU shalt increase my greatness, and comfort me on every side. (Ps. 71:21)

THIS *is* my comfort in my affliction: for thy word hath quickened me. (Ps. 119:50)

THE Spirit of the Lord God *is* upon me; * * *—* * * to comfort all that mourn; (Isa. 61:1,2)

AS one whom his mother comforteth, so will I comfort you; and ye shall be comforted in Jerusalem. (Isa. 66:13)

# GOD IS MY TEACHER

## THERE IS NO FALSE TEACHING

**Bible:**

FOR his God doth instruct him to discretion, *and* doth teach him. (Isa. 28:26)

* * * he will guide you into all truth: * * * (John 16:13)

I WILL instruct thee and teach thee in the way which thou shalt go: * * * (Ps. 32:8)

* * * he will teach us of his ways, * * * (Isa. 2:3)

FOR the Holy Ghost shall teach you * * * (Luke 12:12)

* * * the Comforter, * * * the Holy Ghost, * * * he shall teach you all things, and bring all things to your remembrance, * * * (John 14:26)

# GOD IS MY HOPE

## THERE IS NO DESPAIR

**Bible:**

BE of good courage, and he shall strengthen your heart, all ye that hope in the Lord. (Ps. 31:24)

THEN will I cause you to dwell in this place, in the land that I gave to your fathers, for ever and ever. (Jer. 7:7)

AND now abideth faith, hope, charity, these three; but the greatest of these *is* charity. (I Cor. 13:13)

IF in this life only we have hope in Christ, we are of all men most miserable. (I Cor. 15:19)

TO whom God would make known what *is* the riches of the glory of this mystery among the Gentiles; which is Christ in you, the hope of glory: (Col. 1:27)

# GOD IS MY COMPASSION

## THERE IS NO HARD HEARTEDNESS

**Bible:**

BUT thou, O Lord, *art* a God full of compassion, and gracious, longsuffering, and plenteous in mercy and truth. (Ps. 86:15)

* * * Jesus * * * saith unto him, Go home to thy friends, and tell them how great things the Lord hath done for thee, and hath had compassion on thee. (Mark 5:19)

FINALLY, *be ye* all of one mind, having compassion one of another, love as brethren, *be* pitiful, *be* courteous: (I Peter 3:8)

LET brotherly love continue.—Be not forgetful to entertain strangers: for thereby some have entertained angels unawares. (Heb. 13:1,2)

# GOD IS MY CONTENTMENT

## THERE IS NO DISCONTENT

**Bible:**

A LITTLE that a righteous man hath *is* better than the riches of many wicked. (Ps. 37:16)

REMOVE far from me vanity and lies: give me neither poverty nor riches; feed me with food convenient for me: (Prov. 30:8)

AND having food and raiment let us be therewith content. (I Tim. 6:8)

LET *your* conversation *be* without covetousness; *and be* content with such things as ye have: for he hath said, I will never leave thee, nor forsake thee. (Heb. 13:5)

# GOD IS MY HEARING

## THERE IS NO DEAFNESS

**Bible:**

I HAVE heard of thee by the hearing of the ear: but now mine eye seeth thee. (Job 42:5)

LORD, thou hast heard the desire of the humble: thou wilt prepare their heart, thou wilt cause thine ear to hear: (Ps. 10:17)

HEAR this, all *ye* people; give ear, all *ye* inhabitants of the world:—Both low and high, rich and poor, together. (Ps. 49:1,2)

HE that is of God heareth God's words: * * * (John 8:47)

I WILL hear what God the Lord will speak: * * * (Ps. 85:8)

AND the Lord shall cause his glorious voice to be heard, * * * (Isa. 30:30)

## GOD IS MY PERCEPTION

### THERE IS NO PERPLEXITY

**Bible:**

*** * * it is given unto you to know the mysteries of the kingdom of heaven, * * * (Matt. 13:11)**

HAVING made known unto us the mystery of his will, according to his good pleasure which he hath purposed in himself:—That in the dispensation of the fulness of times he might gather together in one all things in Christ, both which are in heaven, and which are on earth; *even* in him: (Eph. 1:9,10)

BEHOLD, I shew you a mystery; We shall not all sleep, but we shall all be changed,—In a moment, in the twinkling of an eye, * * * (I Cor. 15:51,52)

# GOD IS MY DESIRE

## THERE IS NO CARNALITY

**Bible:**

WHEREFORE laying aside all malice, and all guile, and hypocrisies, and envies, and all evil speakings,—As newborn babes, desire the sincere milk of the word, that ye may grow thereby: (I Peter 2:1,2)

THE statutes of the Lord *are* right, rejoicing the heart: the commandment of the Lord *is* pure, enlightening the eyes. (Ps. 19:8)

ONE *thing* have I desired of the Lord, that will I seek after; that I may dwell in the house of the Lord all the days of my life, to behold the beauty of the Lord, and to enquire in his temple. (Ps. 27:4)

THEREFORE I say unto you, What things soever ye desire, when ye pray, believe that ye receive *them*, and ye shall have *them*. (Mark 11:24)

# GOD IS MY STRENGTH

## THERE IS NO WEAKNESS

**Bible:**

I WILL love thee, O Lord, my strength. (Ps. 18:1)

THE Lord *is* my strength and my shield; my heart trusted in him, and I am helped: * * * (Ps. 28:7)

FOR thou hast been a strength to the poor, a strength to the needy in his distress, a refuge from the storm, a shadow from the heat, when the blast of the terrible ones *is* as a storm *against* the wall. (Isa. 25:4)

TRUST ye in the Lord for ever: for in the Lord JEHOVAH *is* everlasting strength: (Isa. 26:4)

* * * the weakness of God is stronger than men. (I Cor. 1:25)

# GOD IS MY UNDERSTANDING

## THERE IS NO MISCONCEPTION

**Bible:**

THROUGH thy precepts I get understanding: therefore I hate every false way. (Ps. 119:104)

GREAT *is* our Lord, and of great power: his understanding *is* infinite. (Ps. 147:5)

THE Lord by wisdom hath founded the earth; by understanding hath he established the heavens. (Prov. 3:19)

GET wisdom, get understanding: forget *it* not; neither decline from the words of my mouth.—Forsake her not, and she shall preserve thee: love her, and she shall keep thee. (Prov. 4:5,6)

WISDOM *is* before him that hath understanding; * * * (Prov. 17:24)

## GOD IS MY FAITH

### THERE IS NO SKEPTICISM

**Bible:**

* * * verily I say unto you, If ye have faith as a grain of mustard seed, ye shall say unto this mountain, Remove hence to yonder place; and it shall remove; and nothing shall be impossible unto you. (Matt. 17:20)

* * * Verily I say unto you, If ye have faith, and doubt not, ye shall not only do this *which is done* to the fig tree, but also if ye shall say unto this mountain, Be thou removed, and be thou cast into the sea; it shall be done. (Matt. 21:21)

NOW faith is the substance of things hoped for, the evidence of things not seen.—Through faith we understand that the worlds were framed by the word of God, so that things which are seen were not made of things which do appear. (Heb. 11:1,3)

## GOD IS MY ETERNALITY

### THERE IS NO FINITENESS

**Bible:**

THE eternal God *is thy* refuge, and underneath *are* the everlasting arms: and he shall thrust out the enemy from before thee; * * * (Deut. 33:27)

* * * I will make thee an eternal excellency, a joy of many generations. (Isa. 60:15)

AND as Moses lifted up the serpent in the wilderness, even so must the Son of man be lifted up:—That whosoever believeth in him should not perish, but have eternal life. (John 3:14,15)

AND this is life eternal, that they might know thee the only true God, and Jesus Christ, whom thou hast sent. (John 17:3)

## GOD IS MY VICTOR

### THERE IS NO DEFEAT

**Bible:**

THINE, O Lord, *is* the greatness, and the power, and the glory, and the victory, and the majesty: for all *that is* in the heaven and in the earth *is thine*; thine *is* the kingdom, O Lord, and thou art exalted as head above all. (I Chron. 29:11)

* * * Be not afraid nor dismayed by reason of this great multitude; for the battle *is* not your's, but God's. (II Chron. 20:15)

O SING unto the Lord a new song; for he hath done marvellous things: his right hand, and his holy arm, hath gotten him the victory. (Ps. 98:1)

HE will swallow up death in victory; and the Lord God will wipe away tears from off all faces; and the rebuke of his people shall he take away from off all the earth: for the Lord hath spoken *it*. (Isa. 25:8)

# GOD IS MY SAFETY

## THERE IS NO DANGER

**Bible:**

THE fear of man bringeth a snare: but whoso putteth his trust in the Lord shall be safe. (Prov. 29:25)

THEN shalt thou walk in thy way safely, and thy foot shall not stumble. (Prov. 3:23)

BUT whoso hearkeneth unto me shall dwell safely, and shall be quiet from fear of evil. (Prov. 1:33)

HUMBLE yourselves therefore under the mighty hand of God, that he may exalt you in due time:—Casting all your care upon him; for he careth for you. (I Peter 5:6,7)

BE careful for nothing; but in every thing by prayer and supplication with thanksgiving let your requests be made known unto God.—And the peace of God, which passeth all understanding, shall keep your hearts and minds through Christ Jesus. (Phil. 4:6,7)

# GOD IS MY PERFECTION

## THERE IS NO IMPERFECTION

**Bible:**

* * * I *am* the Almighty God; walk before me, and be thou perfect. (Gen. 17:1)

MARK the perfect *man*, and behold the upright: for the end of *that* man *is* peace. (Ps. 37:37)

BUT the path of the just *is* as the shining light, that shineth more and more unto the perfect day. (Prov. 4:18)

BE ye therefore perfect, even as your Father which is in heaven is perfect. (Matt. 5:48)

* * * Be perfect, be of good comfort, be of one mind, live in peace; and the God of love and peace shall be with you. (II Cor. 13:11)

## GOD IS MY POSSESSION

### THERE IS NO DISPOSSESSION

**Bible:**

I LOVE them that love me; and those that seek me early shall find me. (Prov. 8:17)

RICHES and honour *are* with me; *yea,* durable riches and righteousness. (Prov. 8:18)

MY fruit *is* better than gold, yea, than fine gold; and my revenue than choice silver. (Prov. 8:19)

I LEAD in the way of righteousness, in the midst of the paths of judgment: (Prov. 8:20)

THAT I may cause those that love me to inherit substance; and I will fill their treasures. (Prov. 8:21)

THE Lord possessed me in the beginning of his way, before his works of old. (Prov. 8:22)

AND he said unto them, Take heed, and beware of covetousness: for a man's life consisteth not in the abundance of the things which he possesseth. (Luke 12:15)

## GOD IS MY PEACE

### THERE IS NO DISCORD

**Bible:**

ACQUAINT now thyself with him, and be at peace: thereby good shall come unto thee. (Job 22:21)

THE Lord will give strength unto his people; the Lord will bless his people with peace. (Ps. 29:11)

MARK the perfect *man,* and behold the upright: for the end of *that* man *is* peace. (Ps. 37:37)

THOU wilt keep *him* in perfect peace, *whose* mind *is* stayed *on thee:* because he trusteth in thee. (Isa. 26:3)

THEREFORE being justified by faith, we have peace with God through our Lord Jesus Christ: (Rom. 5:1)

# GOD IS MY YOUTHFULNESS

## THERE IS NO OLD AGE

**Bible:**

BLESS the Lord, * * * — Who redeemeth thy life from destruction; who crowneth thee with lovingkindness and tender mercies;—* * * *so that* thy youth is renewed like the eagle's. (Ps. 103:2,4,5)

HE shall pray unto God, and he will be favourable unto him: and he shall see his face with joy: for he will render unto man his righteousness.—His flesh shall be fresher than a child's: he shall return to the days of his youth: (Job 33:26,25)

FOR thou *art* my hope, O Lord God: *thou art* my trust from my youth. (Ps. 71:5)

# GOD IS MY RECTITUDE

## THERE IS NO IMMORALITY

**Bible:**

* * * I have also given thee that which thou has not asked, both riches, and honour: * * * (I Kings 3:13)

WHAT is man, that thou art mindful of him? and the son of man, that thou visitest him?—For thou hast made him a little lower than the angels, and hast crowned him with glory and honour.—Thou madest him to have dominion over the works of thy hands; thou hast put all *things* under his feet: (Ps. 8:4,5,6)

L*ET* love be without dissimulation. Abhor that which is evil; cleave to that which is good. (Rom. 12:9)

B*E* kindly affectioned one to another with brotherly love; in honour preferring one another; (Rom. 12:10)

# GOD IS MY HEAVEN

## THERE IS NO HELL

**Bible:**

WHOM have I in heaven *but thee?* and *there is* none upon earth *that* I desire beside thee. (Ps. 73:25)

FOR who in the heaven can be compared unto the Lord? *who* among the sons of the mighty can be likened unto the Lord? (Ps. 89:6)

UNTO thee lift I up mine eyes, O thou that dwellest in the heavens. (Ps. 123:1)

IN my distress I called upon the Lord, and cried unto my God: he heard my voice out of his temple, * * * (Ps. 18:6)

WHITHER shall I go from thy spirit? or whither shall I flee from thy presence?—If I ascend up into heaven, thou *art* there: if I make my bed in hell, behold, thou *art there.*—Even there shall thy hand lead me, and thy right hand shall hold me. (Ps. 139:7,8,10)

# GOD IS MY VIRTUE

## THERE IS NO WICKEDNESS

**Bible:**

AND they that were vexed with unclean spirits: and they were healed.—And the whole multitude sought to touch him: for there went virtue out of him, and healed *them* all. (Luke 6:18,19)

BLESSED *are* the pure in heart: for they shall see God. (Matt. 5:8)

FINALLY, brethren, whatsoever things are true, whatsoever things *are* honest, whatsoever things *are* just, whatsoever things *are* pure, whatsoever things *are* lovely, whatsoever things *are* of good report; if *there be* any virtue, and if *there be* any praise, think on these things.—And the peace of God, which passeth all understanding, shall keep your hearts and minds through Christ Jesus. (Phil. 4:8,7)

# GOD IS MY POWER

## THERE IS NO IMPOTENCE

**Bible:**

* * * power *belongeth* unto God. (Ps. 62:11)

* * * For thine is the kingdom, and the power, and the glory, for ever. * * * (Matt. 6:13)

BEHOLD, I give unto you power * * * over all the power of the enemy: and nothing shall by any means hurt you. (Luke 10:19)

* * * For there is no power but of God: * * * (Rom. 13:1)

HE giveth power to the faint; and to *them that have* no might he increaseth strength. (Isa. 40:29)

* * * *he is* strong in power; not one faileth. (Isa. 40:26)

# GOD IS MY REFUGE

## THERE IS NO OTHER SHELTER

**Bible:**

TRUST in him at all times; ye people, pour out your heart before him: God *is* a refuge for us. (Ps. 62:8)

* * * *He is* my refuge and my fortress: * * * (Ps. 91:2)

THE eternal God *is thy* refuge, and underneath *are* the everlasting arms: * * * (Deut. 33:27)

THE God of my rock; in him will I trust: *he is* my shield, and the horn of my salvation, my high tower, and my refuge, my saviour; * * * (II Sam. 22:3)

THE Lord also will be a refuge for the oppressed, a refuge in times of trouble. (Ps. 9:9)

GOD *is* our refuge and strength, a very present help in trouble. (Ps. 46:1)

# GOD IS MY FOOD

## THERE IS NO HUNGER

**Bible:**

THEY shall not hunger nor thirst; * * * (Isa. 49:10)

* * * and they shall be no more consumed with hunger in the land, * * * (Eze. 34:29)

AND Jesus said unto them, I am the bread of life: he that cometh to me shall never hunger; * * * (John 6:35)

THEY shall hunger no more, * * * (Rev. 7:16)

FOR the Lord your God *is* God of gods, and Lord of lords, a great God, * * * — He doth execute the judgment of the fatherless and widow, and loveth the stranger, in giving him food and raiment. (Deut. 10:17,18)

# GOD IS MY REDEEMER

## THERE IS NO OTHER REDEMPTION

**Bible:**

I HAVE blotted out, as a thick cloud, thy transgressions, and, as a cloud, thy sins: * * * for I have redeemed thee. (Isa. 44:22)

I WILL ransom them from the power of the grave; I will redeem them from death: * * * (Hos. 13:14)

O GIVE thanks unto the Lord, for *he is* good: for his mercy *endureth* for ever. —Let the redeemed of the Lord say *so*, whom he hath redeemed from the hand of the enemy;—And gathered them out of the lands, from the east, and from the west, from the north, and from the south. (Ps. 107:1,2,3)

FOR I know *that* my redeemer liveth, * * * (Job 19:25)

BLESSED *be* the Lord God of Israel; for he hath visited and redeemed his people, (Luke 1:68)

# GOD IS MY GUIDE

## THERE IS NO MISLEADING

**Bible:**

I WILL instruct thee and teach thee in the way which thou shalt go: I will guide thee with mine eye. (Ps. 32:8)

THE Lord *is* my shepherd; I shall not want. (Ps. 23:1)

FOR this God *is* our God for ever and ever: he will be our guide *even* unto death. (Ps. 48:14)

THOU shalt guide me with thy counsel, and afterward receive me *to* glory. (Ps. 73:24)

AND the Lord shall guide thee continually, * * * (Isa. 58:11)

* * * he will guide you into all truth: * * * (John 16:13)

* * * thou thyself art a guide of the blind, a light of them which are in darkness, (Rom. 2:19)

# GOD IS MY DEFENCE

## THERE IS NO ADVERSARY

**Bible:**

FOR the Lord *is* our defence; * * * (Ps. 89:18)

THE enemy shall not exact upon him; nor the son of wickedness afflict him. (Ps. 89:22)

FOR the nation and kingdom that will not serve thee shall perish; yea, *those* nations shall be utterly wasted. (Isa. 60:12)

FOR thou hast been a shelter for me, *and* a strong tower from the enemy. (Ps. 61:3)

HE only *is* my rock and my salvation; *he is* my defence; * * * (Ps. 62:2)

THE last enemy *that* shall be destroyed *is* death. (I Cor. 15:26)

## GOD IS MY SECURITY

### THERE IS NO JEOPARDY

**Bible:**

AND this is the Father's will * * * that of all which he hath given me I should lose nothing, * * * (John 6:39)

AND *thine* age shall be clearer than the noonday; thou shalt shine forth, thou shalt be as the morning.—And thou shalt be secure, * * * (Job 11:17,18)

BUT whoso hearkeneth unto me shall dwell safely, and shall be quiet from fear of evil. (Prov. 1:33)

THE fear of man bringeth a snare: but whoso putteth his trust in the Lord shall be safe. (Prov. 29:25)

## GOD IS MY CONFIDENCE

### THERE IS NO DOUBT NOR FEAR

**Bible:**

BE not afraid of sudden fear, neither of the desolation of the wicked, when it cometh.—For the Lord shall be thy confidence, and shall keep thy foot from being taken. (Prov. 3:25,26)

AND now, little children, abide in him; that, when he shall appear, we may have confidence, and not be ashamed before him at his coming. (I John 2:28)

BELOVED, if our heart condemn us not, *then* have we confidence toward God. (I John 3:21)

AND this is the confidence that we have in him, that, if we ask any thing according to his will, he heareth us: (I John 5:14)

## GOD IS MY PHYSICIAN

### THERE IS NO OTHER HEALER

**Bible:**

* * * I *am* the Lord that healeth thee. (Ex. 15:26)

* * * who healeth all thy diseases; (Ps. 103:3)

HE healeth the broken in heart, and bindeth up their wounds. (Ps. 147:3)

FOR I will restore health unto thee, and I will heal thee of thy wounds, saith the Lord; * * * (Jer. 30:17)

BEHOLD, I will bring it health and cure, and I will cure them, * * * (Jer. 33:6)

THEN the eyes of the blind shall be opened, and the ears of the deaf shall be unstopped.—Then shall the lame *man* leap as an hart, and the tongue of the dumb sing: * * * (Isa. 35:5,6)

## GOD IS MY REST

### THERE IS NO WEARINESS NOR INSOMNIA

**Bible:**

* * * My presence shall go *with thee,* and I will give thee rest. (Ex. 33:14)

AND my people shall dwell in a peaceable habitation, and in sure dwellings, and in quiet resting places; (Isa. 32:18)

WHEN thou liest down, thou shalt not be afraid: yea, thou shalt lie down, and thy sleep shall be sweet. (Prov. 3:24)

COME unto me, all *ye* that labour and are heavy laden, and I will give you rest. (Matt. 11:28)

THERE remaineth therefore a rest to the people of God. (Heb. 4:9)

# GOD IS MY RELIGION

## THERE IS NO APOSTASY

**Bible:**

IF any man among you seem to be religious, and bridleth not his tongue, but deceiveth his own heart, this man's religion *is* vain.—Pure religion and undefiled before God and the Father is this, To visit the fatherless and widows in their affliction, *and* to keep himself unspotted from the world. (James 1:26,27)

HEAR, ye children, the instruction of a father, and attend to know understanding.—For I give you good doctrine, forsake ye not my law. (Prov. 4:1,2)

JESUS answered them, and said, My doctrine is not mine, but his that sent me. —If any man will do his will, he shall know of the doctrine, whether it be of God, or *whether* I speak of myself. (John 7:16,17)

## GOD IS MY AFFECTION

### THERE IS NO DISAFFECTION

**Bible:**

LORD, I have loved the habitation of thy house, and the place where thine honour dwelleth. (Ps. 26:8)

MY soul longeth, yea, even fainteth for the courts of the Lord: my heart and my flesh crieth out for the living God. (Ps. 84:2)

SET your affection on things above, not on things on the earth. (Col. 3:2)

T*HIS* I say then, Walk in the Spirit, and ye shall not fulfill the lust of the flesh. (Gal. 5:16)

AND they that are Christ's have crucified the flesh with the affections and lusts. (Gal. 5:24)

# GOD IS MY REWARD

## THERE IS NO LACK OF COMPENSATION

**Bible:**

BLESSED *is* the man that endureth temptation: for when he is tried, he shall receive the crown of life, which the Lord hath promised to them that love him. (James 1:12)

* * * he is a rewarder of them that diligently seek him. (Heb. 11:6)

AND they shall build houses, and inhabit *them;* and they shall plant vineyards, and eat the fruit of them.—They shall not build, and another inhabit; they shall not plant, and another eat: for as the days of a tree *are* the days of my people, and mine elect shall long enjoy the work of their hands.—They shall not labour in vain, nor bring forth for trouble; for they *are* the seed of the blessed of the Lord, and their offspring with them.—And it shall come to pass, that before they call, I will answer; and while they are yet speaking, I will hear. (Isa. 65:21-24)

# GOD IS MY OPPORTUNITY

## THERE IS NO LOST OPPORTUNITY

**Bible:**

FOR he that soweth to his flesh shall of the flesh reap corruption; but he that soweth to the Spirit shall of the Spirit reap life everlasting.—And let us not be weary in well doing: for in due season we shall reap, if we faint not.—As we have therefore opportunity, let us do good unto all *men,* especially unto them who are of the household of faith. (Gal. 6:8,9,10)

FOR the Lord of hosts hath purposed, and who shall disannul *it?* * * * (Isa. 14:27)

AND we know that all things work together for good to them that love God, to them who are the called according to *his* purpose. (Rom. 8:28)

IN whom also we have obtained an inheritance, being predestinated according to the purpose of him who worketh all things after the counsel of his own will: (Eph. 1:11)

# GOD IS MY EMPLOYER

## THERE IS NO UNEMPLOYMENT

**Bible:**

I CAN of mine own self do nothing: * * * —* * * the Father that dwelleth in me, he doeth the works. (John 5:30—John 14:10)

THE works of the Lord *are* great, sought out of all them that have pleasure therein.—His work *is* honourable and glorious: and his righteousness endureth for ever. (Ps. 111:2,3)

FOR all this I considered in my heart even to declare all this, that the righteous, and the wise, and their works, *are* in the hand of God: * * * (Eccl. 9:1)

* * * I have spent my strength for nought, and in vain: *yet* surely my judgment *is* with the Lord, and my work with my God. (Isa. 49:4)

# GOD IS MY BUSINESS

## THERE IS NO OTHER VOCATION NOR PROFESSION

**Bible:**

SEEST thou a man diligent in his business? he shall stand before kings; he shall not stand before mean *men.* (Prov. 22:29)

* * * wist ye not that I must be about my Father's business? (Luke 2:49)

L*ET* love be without dissimulation. Abhor that which is evil; cleave to that which is good.—*Be* kindly affectioned one to another with brotherly love; in honour preferring one another;—Not slothful in business; fervent in spirit; serving the Lord;—Rejoicing in hope; patient in tribulation; continuing instant in prayer; (Rom. 12:9,10,11,12)

# GOD IS MY MEMORY

## THERE IS NO CONFUSION NOR AMNESIA

**Bible:**

GREAT *is* the Lord, and greatly to be praised; and his greatness *is* unsearchable.—They shall abundantly utter the memory of thy great goodness, and shall sing of thy righteousness.—The Lord *is* good to all: and his tender mercies *are* over all his works. (Ps. 145:3,7,9)

THE memory of the just *is* blessed: * * * (Prov. 10:7)

WHAT is man, that thou art mindful of him? and the son of man, that thou visitest him?—For thou hast made him a little lower than the angels, and hast crowned him with glory and honour.—Thou madest him to have dominion over the works of thy hands; thou hast put all *things* under his feet: (Ps. 8:4,5,6)

# GOD IS MY SIGHT

## THERE IS NO IMPERFECT VISION

**Bible:**

* * * And the Lord opened the eyes of the young man; and he saw: * * * (II Kings 6:17)

FOR mine eyes have seen thy salvation,—Which thou hast prepared before the face of all people;—A light to lighten the Gentiles, and the glory of thy people Israel. (Luke 2:30,31,32)

THE light of the body is the eye: therefore when thine eye is single, thy whole body also is full of light; but when *thine eye* is evil, thy body also *is* full of darkness. (Luke 11:34)

# GOD IS MY GOODNESS

## THERE IS NO BADNESS

**Bible:**

* * * The Lord, The Lord God, merciful and gracious, longsuffering, and abundant in goodness and truth, (Ex. 34:6)

SURELY goodness and mercy shall follow me all the days of my life: and I will dwell in the house of the Lord for ever. (Ps. 23:6)

I *HAD fainted,* unless I had believed to see the goodness of the Lord in the land of the living. (Ps. 27:13)

OH how great *is* thy goodness, which thou hast laid up for them that fear thee; *which* thou hast wrought for them that trust in thee before the sons of men! (Ps. 31:19)

* * * the earth is full of the goodness of the Lord. (Ps. 33:5)

# GOD IS MY DEPORTMENT

## THERE IS NO MISCONDUCT

**Bible:**

BUT as he which hath called you is holy, so be ye holy in all manner of conversation; (I Peter 1:15)

SEEING then *that* all these things shall be dissolved, what manner *of persons* ought ye to be in *all* holy conversation and godliness,—Nevertheless we, according to his promise, look for new heavens and a new earth, wherein dwelleth righteousness. (II Peter 3:11,13)

GIVE unto the Lord the glory due unto his name; worship the Lord in the beauty of holiness. (Ps. 29:2)

TEACH me thy way, O Lord, and lead me in a plain path, * * * (Ps. 27:11)

# GOD IS MY RULER

## THERE IS NO MATERIAL RULER

**Bible:**

AND Gideon said unto them, I will not rule over you, neither shall my son rule over you: the Lord shall rule over you. (Judges 8:23)

COUNSEL *is* mine, and sound wisdom: I *am* understanding; I have strength.—By me kings reign, and princes decree justice.—By me princes rule, and nobles, *even* all the judges of the earth. (Prov. 8:14,15, 16)

BEHOLD, the Lord God will come with strong *hand,* and his arm shall rule for him: * * * —He shall feed his flock like a shepherd: he shall gather the lambs with his arm, and carry *them* in his bosom, *and* shall gently lead those that are with young. (Isa. 40:10,11)

# GOD IS MY BREATH OF LIFE

## THERE IS NO MATERIAL ATMOSPHERE

**Bible:**

WHO knoweth not in all these that the hand of the Lord hath wrought this? —In whose hand *is* the soul of every living thing, and the breath of all mankind. (Job 12:9,10)

THE Spirit of God hath made me, and the breath of the Almighty hath given me life. (Job 33:4)

* * * the God in whose hand thy breath *is*, and whose *are* all thy ways, hast thou not glorified: (Dan. 5:23)

GOD that made the world and all things therein, * * * — * * * giveth to all life, and breath, and all things; (Acts 17:24,25)

# GOD IS MY PRESENCE

## THERE IS NO ABSENCE

**Bible:**

* * * My presence shall go *with thee,* and I will give thee rest. (Ex. 33:14)

THOU wilt shew me the path of life: in thy presence *is* fulness of joy; at thy right hand *there are* pleasures for evermore. (Ps. 16:11)

WHITHER shall I go from thy spirit? or whither shall I flee from thy presence? (Ps. 139:7)

FOR Christ is not entered into the holy places made with hands, *which are* the figures of the true; but into heaven itself, now to appear in the presence of God for us: (Heb. 9:24)

# GOD IS MY ATTRACTION

## THERE IS NO ANIMAL MAGNETISM

**Bible:**

DRAW me not away with the wicked, * * * (Ps. 28:3)

BUT *it is* good for me to draw near to God: I have put my trust in the Lord God, that I may declare all thy works. (Ps. 73:28)

* * * If thou knewest the gift of God, and who it is that saith to thee, Give me to drink; thou wouldest have asked of him, and he would have given thee living water. (John 4:10)

NO man can come to me, except the Father which hath sent me draw him: * * * (John 6:44)

AND I, if I be lifted up from the earth, will draw all *men* unto me. (John 12:32)

# GOD IS MY INSPIRATION

## THERE IS NO OTHER INFLUENCE

**Bible:**

BUT *there is* a spirit in man: and the inspiration of the Almighty giveth them understanding. (Job 32:8)

FOR truly my words *shall* not *be* false: he that is perfect in knowledge *is* with thee. (Job 36:4)

O LORD, thou *art* my God; I will exalt thee, I will praise thy name; for thou hast done wonderful *things; thy* counsels of old *are* faithfulness *and* truth. (Isa. 25:1)

* * * I *am* the Lord thy God which teacheth thee to profit, which leadeth thee by the way *that* thou shouldest go. (Isa. 48:17)

NOW we have received, not the spirit of the world, but the spirit which is of God; that we might know the things that are freely given to us of God. (I Cor. 2:12)

## GOD IS MY FIDELITY

### THERE IS NO DISLOYALTY

**Bible:**

THY word *is* true *from* the beginning: and every one of thy righteous judgments *endureth* for ever. (Ps. 119:160)

THY faithfulness *is* unto all generations: thou hast established the earth, and it abideth. (Ps. 119:90)

* * * the hour cometh, and now is, when the true worshippers shall worship the Father in spirit and in truth: for the Father seeketh such to worship him. (John 4:23)

SHADRACH, Meshach, and Abed-nego, answered and said to the king, O Nebuchadnezzar, we *are* not careful to answer thee in this matter.—* * * our God whom we serve is able to deliver us from the burning fiery furnace, and he will deliver *us* out of thine hand, O king. (Dan. 3:16,17)

## GOD IS MY HEART

### THERE IS NO HEART FAILURE

**Bible:**

BE of good courage, and he shall strengthen your heart, all ye that hope in the Lord. (Ps. 31:24)

THE law of his God *is* in his heart; none of his steps shall slide. (Ps. 37:31)

* * * God *is* the strength of my heart, and my portion for ever. (Ps. 73:26)

MY heart is fixed, O God, my heart is fixed: I will sing and give praise. (Ps. 57:7)

THE meek shall eat and be satisfied: they shall praise the Lord that seek him: your heart shall live for ever. (Ps. 22:26)

## GOD IS MY TREASURE

### THERE IS NO OTHER VALUE

**Bible:**

FOR where your treasure is, there will your heart be also. (Matt. 6:21)

THE Lord shall open unto thee his good treasure, the heaven to give the rain unto thy land in his season, and to bless all the work of thine hand: * * * (Deut. 28:12)

IN the house of the righteous *is* much treasure: * * * (Prov. 15:6)

BRING ye all the tithes into the storehouse, that there may be meat in mine house, and prove me now herewith, saith the Lord of hosts, if I will not open you the windows of heaven, and pour you out a blessing, that *there shall* not *be room* enough *to receive it.* (Mal. 3:10)

# GOD IS MY HEALTH

## THERE IS NO DISEASE

**Bible:**

* * * hope thou in God: for I shall yet praise him, ***who is*** the health of my countenance, and my God. (Ps. 42:11)

BLESS the Lord, O my soul, and forget not all his benefits:—Who forgiveth all thine iniquities; who healeth all thy diseases; (Ps. 103:2,3)

THEN shall thy light break forth as the morning, and thine health shall spring forth speedily: and thy righteousness shall go before thee; the glory of the Lord shall by thy rereward. (Isa. 58:8)

FOR I will restore health unto thee, and I will heal thee of thy wounds, saith the Lord; * * * (Jer. 30:17)

## GOD IS MY ABILITY

### THERE IS NO INABILITY NOR DISABILITY

**Bible:**

* * * I thank Christ Jesus our Lord, who hath enabled me, for that he counted me faithful, putting me into the ministry; (I Tim. 1:12)

FOR since the beginning of the world *men* have not heard, nor perceived by the ear, neither hath the eye seen, O God, beside thee, *what* he hath prepared for him that waiteth for him. (Isa. 64:4)

IN whom also we have obtained an inheritance, being predestinated according to the purpose of him who worketh all things after the counsel of his own will: (Eph. 1:11)

NOW unto him that is able to do exceeding abundantly above all that we ask or think, according to the power that worketh in us,—Unto him *be* glory in the church by Christ Jesus throughout all ages, world without end. (Eph. 3:20,21)

# GOD IS MY MASTER

## THERE IS NO SLAVERY

**Bible:**

WHOSO keepeth the fig tree shall eat the fruit thereof: so he that waiteth on his master shall be honoured. (Prov. 27:18)

THE disciple is not above *his* master, nor the servant above his lord.—It is enough for the disciple that he be as his master, and the servant as his lord. * * * (Matt. 10:24,25)

* * * one is your Master, *even* Christ; and all ye are brethren. (Matt. 23:8)

AND the scribe said unto him, Well, Master, thou hast said the truth: for there is one God; and there is none other but he: —And to love him with all the heart, and with all the understanding, and with all the soul, and with all the strength, and to love *his* neighbour as himself, is more than all whole burnt offerings and sacrifices. (Mark 12:32,33)

## GOD IS MY WORSHIP

### THERE IS NO IDOLATRY

**Bible:**

FOR thou shalt worship no other god: * * * (Ex. 34:14)

GIVE unto the Lord the glory due unto his name; worship the Lord in the beauty of holiness. (Ps. 29:2)

ALL the earth shall worship thee, and shall sing unto thee; they shall sing *to* thy name. (Ps. 66:4)

THERE shall no strange god be in thee; neither shalt thou worship any strange god. (Ps. 81:9)

ALL nations whom thou hast made shall come and worship before thee, O Lord; and shall glorify thy name. (Ps. 86:9)

## GOD IS MY SAVIOUR

### THERE IS NO DESTROYER

**Bible:**

FOR I *am* the Lord thy God, the Holy One of Israel, thy Saviour: * * * (Isa. 43:3)

FEAR not: for I *am* with thee: I will bring thy seed from the east, and gather thee from the west; (Isa. 43:5)

FOR he said, Surely they *are* my people, children *that* will not lie: so he was their Saviour. (Isa. 63:8)

AND my spirit hath rejoiced in God my Saviour. (Luke 1:47)

O MAGNIFY the Lord with me, and let us exalt his name together.—I sought the Lord, and he heard me, and delivered me from all my fears. (Ps. 34:3,4)

# GOD IS MY CHURCH

## THERE IS NO FALSE THEOLOGY

**Bible:**

**TAKE heed therefore unto yourselves, and to all the flock, over the which the Holy Ghost hath made you overseers, to feed the church of God, * * * (Acts 20:28)**

**AND now, brethren, I commend you to God, and to the word of his grace, which is able to build you up, and to give you an inheritance among all them which are sanctified. (Acts 20:32)**

**AND what *is* the exceeding greatness of his power to us-ward who believe, according to the working of his mighty power,—Which he wrought in Christ, when he raised him from the dead, and set *him* at his own right hand in the heavenly *places*,—And hath put all *things* under his feet, and gave him *to be* the head over all *things* to the church,—Which is his body, the fulness of him that filleth all in all (Eph. 1:19,20,22,23)**

# GOD IS MY PLACE

## THERE IS NO MISPLACEMENT

**Bible:**

* * * the place whereon thou standest *is* holy ground. (Ex. 3:5)

THOU *art* my hiding place; thou shalt preserve me from trouble; thou shalt compass me about with songs of deliverance. (Ps. 32:7)

IN the fear of the Lord *is* strong confidence: and his children shall have a place of refuge. (Pro. 14:26)

BLESSED *be* the God and Father of our Lord Jesus Christ, who hath blessed us with all spiritual blessings in heavenly *places* in Christ: (Eph. 1:3)

AND hath raised *us* up together, and made *us* sit together in heavenly *places* in Christ Jesus: (Eph. 2:6)

# GOD IS MY TRANSPORTATION

## THERE IS NO DELAY NOR ACCIDENT

**Bible:**

* * * they willingly received him into the ship: and immediately the ship was at the land whither they went. (John 6:21)

AND in the fourth watch of the night Jesus went unto them, walking on the sea.—And when the disciples saw him walking on the sea, they were troubled, saying, It is a spirit; and they cried out for fear.—But straightway Jesus spake unto them, saying, Be of good cheer; it is I; be not afraid.—And Peter answered him and said, Lord, if it be thou, bid me come unto thee on the water.—And he said, Come. And when Peter was come down out of the ship, he walked on the water, to go to Jesus.—But when he saw the wind boisterous, he was afraid; and beginning to sink, he cried, saying, Lord, save me.—And immediately Jesus stretched forth *his* hand, and caught him, and said unto him, O thou of little faith, wherefore didst thou doubt? (Matt. 14:25-31)

# GOD IS MY BODILY FORM

## THERE IS NO OBESITY, EMACIATION NOR MALFORMATION

**Bible:**

FOR in him dwelleth all the fulness of the Godhead bodily. (Col. 2:9)

WHAT? know ye not that your body is the temple of the Holy Ghost *which is* in you, which ye have of God, and ye are not your own? (I Cor. 6:19)

FOR we know that if our earthly house of *this* tabernacle were dissolved, we have a building of God, an house not made with hands, eternal in the heavens. (II Cor. 5:1)

* * * Take no thought for your life, what ye shall eat; neither for the body, what ye shall put on.—The life is more than meat, and the body *is more* than raiment. (Luke 12:22,23)

BUT refuse profane and old wives' fables, and exercise thyself *rather* unto godliness.—For bodily exercise profiteth little: but godliness is profitable unto all things, * * * (I Tim. 4:7,8)

# GOD IS MY BEING

## THERE IS NO OTHER SELF

**Bible:**

ALL things were made by him; and without him was not any thing made that was made.—In him was life; and the life was the light of men. (John 1:3,4)

FOR God is my witness, whom I serve with my spirit in the gospel of his Son, * * * (Rom. 1:9)

* * * Christ liveth in me: and the life which I now live in the flesh I live by the faith of the Son of God, * * * —I do not frustrate the grace of God: * * * (Gal. 2: 20,21)

AND now, O Father, glorify thou me with thine own self with the glory which I had with thee before the world was. (John 17:5)

Other helpful acknowledgments of
God appear on the follow-
ing pages

God is my Patience;
There is no agitation.

God is my Spontaneity;
There is no constraint.

God is my Success;
There is no failure.

God is my Progress;
There is no retrogression.

God is my Occupation;
There is no idleness.

God is my Home;
There is no exile.

God is my Motive;
There is no ulterior motive.

God is my Stature;
There is no abnormality.

God is my Appearance;
There is no unsightliness.

God is my Gratitude;
There is no ingratitude.

God is my Wakefulness;
There is no drowsiness nor
hypnotism.

God is my Life-Blood;
There is no anæmia.

God is my Ego;
There is no egotism.

God is my Honesty;
There is no dishonesty.

God is my Activity;
There is no abnormal action.

God is my Purity;
There is no corruption.

God is my Expectation;
There is no disappointment.

God is my Investment;
There is no risk.

God is my Alertness;
There is no inertia.

God is my Abundance;
There is no deficiency.

God is my Beauty;
There is no ugliness.

God is my Counselor;
There is no other advisor.

God is my Capacity;
There is no incapacity.

God is my Vitality;
There is no infirmity.

# CONCLUSION

The declarations of truth in this booklet must indicate to the reader the numberless ways by which the inspired Word of the Bible may be made practical when its divine purpose is fully comprehended.

# INDEX TO TEXTS

# INDEX — *Continued*

www.ingramcontent.com/pod-product-compliance
Lightning Source LLC
Chambersburg PA
CBHW031812110525
26507CB00099B/195

* 9 7 8 1 4 3 2 5 6 1 7 9 6 *